Simple Machines

Grades 1-3

Written by Paul and Clare Reid
Illustrated by Sean Parkes and S&S Learning Materials

ISBN 1-55035-586-4
Copyright 1998
Revised January 2006
All Rights Reserved * Printed in Canada

Published in the United States by:
On the Mark Press
3909 Witmer Road PMB 175
Niagara Falls, New York
14305
www.onthemarkpress.com

Published in Canada by:
S&S Learning Materials
15 Dairy Avenue
Napanee, Ontario
K7R 1M4
www.sslearning.com

At  Glance™

Learning Expectations	Science Experiments							
	Inclined PLane	The Wedge	The Screw	Levers	The Pulley	Wheel & Axle	Work Sheets & Activities	Invention Fair
Understanding Concepts								
• Describe different mechanisms through observation and investigation (e.g., inclined plane), and identify the components that are simple machines (e.g., lever, wedge)	•	•	•	•	•	•		
• Describe, through observations, characteristics and movements of simple machines	•	•	•	•	•	•		
• Describe the changes in the amount of effort needed to lift, push or pull a load with and without the use of a simple machine	•				•			
• Describe the effects of changing the slope of an inclined plane on the motion of the object that is placed on it (e.g., change in distance traveled)	•							
• Describe the changes in the amount of turns needed when the pitch of a screw is changed			•					
• Describe the changes in the amount of effort needed to lift a load with a lever when the position of the fulcrum is changed				•				
• Describe the changes in the amount of effort needed to turn a wheel when the diameter of the axle is changed						•		
• Describe how the parts of some systems work together (e.g., wheel and axle, pulley and string)					•	•		
Skills of Inquiry, Design & Communication								
• Demonstrate an awareness of the scientific method	•	•	•	•	•	•		
• Use appropriate vocabulary to describe investigations, explorations, and observations	•	•	•	•	•	•	•	•
• Construct a simple machine					•			
• Design and make an invention, and participate in an invention fair								•
• Record observations, findings and measurements using drawings, charts, and written descriptions	•	•	•	•	•	•		•
• Communicate the procedures and results of investigations using drawings and oral and written descriptions	•	•	•	•	•	•		•
• Recognize and apply science safety procedures in the classroom	•	•	•	•	•	•	•	
Relating Science & Technology to the World Outside of the School								
• Identify simple machines in the immediate environment and the world	•	•	•	•	•	•	•	
• Explain the function of a structure that students have made, and describe how they made it								•
Language & Creativity								
• Cloze activity, write an acrostic poem, create a riddle, imagine a machine of the future, make an idea web, create a collage							•	

SIMPLE
MACHINES

Table of Contents

At A Glance™ 2

Teacher Assessment Rubric 4

Student Self-Assessment Rubric 5

Teacher Suggestions 6

Scientific Method - for Teachers 7

Scientific Method - for Students 9

Simple Machines - Experiments and Activities

    Inclined Plane 10

    The Wedge 17

    The Screw... 22

    Levers 29

    The Pulley 38

    Wheel and Axle 45

    Compound Machines 51

Student Learning Log 53

Student Review Work Sheets 62

Student Follow-Up Activities and Work Sheets 65

Invention Fair 84

Invention Conference Form 88

Certificate of Completion 89

Blank Form for Student Groupings 90

Teacher-Student Conference Form 91

Blank Activity Sheets 92

Answer Key 94

Teacher Assessment Rubric

Student's Name: _____

Criteria	Level 1	Level 2	Level 3	Level 4	Level
Understanding Concepts					
• Demonstrated understanding of the basic concepts of inclined plane, wedge, screw, lever, pulley, wheel & axle, and compound machines	Limited	Some	General	Thorough	
• Characteristics of demonstrated misconceptions	Significant misconceptions	Minor misconceptions	No significant misconceptions	No misconceptions	
• Characteristics of explanations that were given	Shows limited understanding of concepts	Only partial explanations given	Usually complete or almost complete	Always complete and accurate	
Inquiry & Communication Skills					
• Ability to apply the skills and strategies of questioning, prediction, procedure, observations and conclusion as they relate to the scientific method	Limited	Some	Good	Consistent	
• Use of the correct vocabulary relating to simple machines, and clarity and precision of communication	Limited	Some	Good	Consistent	
• Awareness and use of safety procedures in the classroom	Limited	Some	Good	Consistent	
Relating Science & Technology to Each Other and the World Outside of School					
• Demonstrated understanding of the connections between the science and technology of simple machines in familiar contexts (home, school, etc.)	Limited	Some	Demonstrates understanding	Understands connections in familiar and unfamiliar contexts	
• Demonstrated understanding of the connections between the science and technology of simple machines and the world	Limited	Some	Demonstrates understanding	Understands connections and their implications	
Language & Creativity					
• Evidence of thoughtfulness and creativity in responses, and invention design and construction	Limited	Some	Good	Consistent	

SIMPLE MACHINES

Student Self-Assessment Rubric

Name: _____

Put a check mark (✓) in the box that best describes you.

	Always ☆ ☆ ☆ ☆	Almost Always ☆ ☆ ☆	Sometimes ☆ ☆	Needs Improvement ☆
✓ I am a good listener.				
✓ I followed the directions.				
✓ I stayed on task and finished my work on time.				
✓ I remembered safety when I used tools and equipment.				
✓ My writing is neat and accurate.				
✓ My pictures are neat and colored.				
✓ I know what I am good at.				
✓ I know what I need to work on.				

1. I liked _____

_____

2. I learned _____

_____

3. I want to learn _____

_____

SIMPLE MACHINES

Teacher Suggestions

- The teacher should become very familiar with the six specified simple machines and how they work.

- Introduce the Scientific Method (p. 7) to the class before attempting experiments. Post the student list page as a reminder (p. 9).

- Collect all materials required for the experiments and try the experiments before introducing them to the class.

- Exchange any of the materials required for experiments with suitable items that are available to you.

- Discuss science safety issues with the students before completing experiments. Be a good role model for them in the classroom.

- Encourage the students to ask their own questions and attempt to answer them through experimentation.

- Always point out practical examples to the students when discussing simple machines.

- Whenever possible, allow the students the opportunity to experience and learn through a "hands on" approach.

- Select the activities which meet the needs of the individual students.

- You may choose to use the structured Scientific Method experiment sheets or the Learning Log (p. 53) for student response and evaluation.

- Encourage parental involvement throughout the Invention Fair process.

Scientific Method for Teachers

The **Scientific Method** is an investigative process which follows a logical progression of steps to discover if evidence supports a hypothesis. This is an excellent set of procedures for the beginning scientist to follow.

1   Consider a **question** to investigate.

After asking a question, it is necessary to find resources before you can investigate. It is important to choose a question that is clear and one that the students are capable of answering.

Example: *Does air take up space?*

2   **Predict** what you think will happen, or identify your hypothesis.

A hypothesis is an educated guess about the answer to the question being investigated.

Example: *I believe air does take up space.*

3   Create a plan or **procedure** to investigate the hypothesis.

In devising a plan or set of procedures, the students must make a list of materials that will be required during their investigations. A numbered set of instructions must be written and strictly followed.

SIMPLE
MACHINES

Scientific Method for Teachers

---

4   Record all of the **observations** of the investigation.

It is very important that all observations be recorded in a data journal so that future investigations can benefit from those of the past. Results should be recorded in written and picture form.

> **Example:** *Water did not enter the glass and the paper remained dry.*

5   Write a **conclusion**.

A conclusion is a statement which summarizes the findings of the investigation, and indicates whether the findings support or do not support the hypothesis. It is important to relate the experiment results to the hypothesis stated at the outset of the process.

> **Example:** *The results of the experiment support my original hypothesis that air takes up space.*

It is very important that the students be taught to accurately record results in their data journal on a daily basis. This journal can therefore be used by others to assist them or to continue the investigation. Any comments, observations or planned investigations in the future should also be noted.

Scientific Method for Students

The Scientific Method is a series of logical, progressive steps used to find out if evidence supports a prediction. This is an excellent set of procedures for the beginning scientist to follow.

1   **I wonder** - Think of a question to investigate.

2   **I think** - Predict what you think will happen.

3   **I will** - List the steps you plan to follow.

4   **I saw** - Write down what you saw, and draw a picture.

5   **I learned** - Tell whether or not the results of the experiment support your prediction.

Inclined Plane

Name: _____

The **inclined plane** is a sloping surface which allows an object to be moved from one elevation to another with less effort than lifting. Using an inclined plane requires **less work**, but effort occurs over a **greater distance**. Pushing or pulling the object using an inclined plane is easier than lifting the object. Color each inclined plane below.

Inclined Plane

Experiment One

Question: Does an inclined plane make lifting easier?

Materials Required:
- two shoe boxes
- a one-meter (one-yard) string or rope
- a one- to two-meter (three- to six-foot) board
- several weights of equal mass
- a student desk
- a meter stick (yard stick)

Procedure: **Part 1**

1. Fasten the string or rope to the shoe boxes. Label them Box A and Box B.
2. Place Box A on the floor and hang Box B over the desk.
3. Begin to place weights into Box B until Box A begins to lift upward.
4. Continue until Box A reaches the top of the desk.
5. Measure the distance from the floor to the top of the desk.
6. Record the amount of weight required to lift Box A.

Part 2

7. Place one end of the board on the floor and the other end on the desk.
8. Repeat steps 1 to 4, but this time Box A should be placed on the board to begin.
9. Measure the distance the box traveled on the board.
10. Compare the amount of weight required to lift Box A to the same elevation of the desk, with and without the use of an inclined plane. Compare the distance traveled.

Conclusion: The students will discover that less weight is required to lift the box using an inclined plane. Have the students complete the student experiment sheet (p. 13). Ensure the students include a diagram.

Inclined Plane

Experiment One

Part 1

Part 2

Inclined Plane

Name: _____

Experiment One

I wonder: _____

_____

_____

I think: _____

_____

_____

I will: _____

_____

_____

_____

I saw: _____

_____

_____

_____

I learned: _____

_____

_____

SIMPLE MACHINES

Inclined Plane

Experiment Two

Question: Does increasing or decreasing the slope of an inclined plane change the amount of effort required to lift an object?

Materials Required:

- two shoe boxes
- string or rope (length will vary)
- several boards of varying lengths
- several weights of equal mass
- a student desk
- a meter stick (yard stick)

Procedure:
1. Measure the lengths of the boards and record them.
2. Fasten the string or rope to the shoe boxes. Label them Box A and Box B.
3. Place one end of the shortest board on the floor and the other end on the desk.
4. Place Box A on the lower end of the board and hang Box B over the desk.
5. Begin to place weights in to Box B until Box A begins to lift upward.
6. Continue until Box A reaches the top of the desk.
7. Record the amount of weight required to lift Box A.
8. Repeat steps 1 to 7 using another length of board.
9. Compare the amount of weight required to lift Box A to the same elevation of the desk, using inclined planes of different slopes. Compare the distance traveled.
10. Discuss the results with the class.

Conclusion: The students will discover that the greater slope requires less effort to lift an object, but the object will travel a greater distance.

Ensure the students complete the student experiment sheet. Have the students include a diagram.

Inclined Plane

Experiment Two

Inclined Plane

Name: _____

Experiment Two

I wonder: _____

_____

_____

I think: _____

_____

_____

I will: _____

_____

_____

_____

I saw: _____

_____

_____

_____

I learned: _____

_____

_____

The Wedge

Name: _____

A **wedge** is an inclined plane that **moves**. It is thin at one end and thicker at the other end. A wedge can lift something, or split something apart. Wedges are usually made of wood or metal. Color each wedge below.

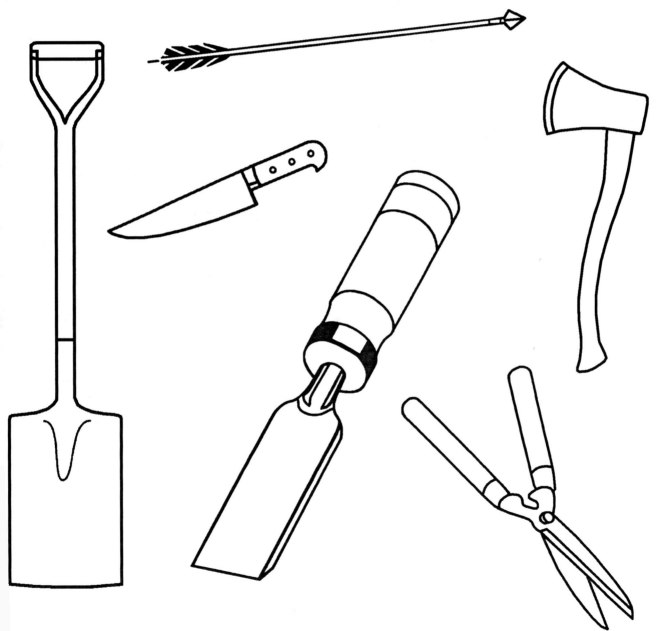

SIMPLE MACHINES

The Wedge

Experiment One

Question: How is a wedge used?

Materials Required:
- a door stop
- a block of wood
- a shovel
- a knife
- a carrot
- a hammer

Procedure: Part 1

1. Place a block of wood against an open door.
2. Ask a student to close the door.
3. Place a door stop (wedge) under the door.
4. Ask a student to close the door.
5. Discuss why it was more difficult to close the door when using the doorstop.

Part 2

6. Using a knife like a saw, try to cut a cross-section of a carrot.
7. Place the knife across the carrot and strike the back of the knife with a hammer.
8. Discuss which method was the most effective to cut the carrot.

Part 3

9. Take the class out into the schoolyard.
10. Choose one student to dig the shovel into the ground.
11. Discuss how the shovel worked and the amount of force required.

The Wedge

Experiment One

Conclusion: The doorstop raises the door, therefore making it very difficult to close. The further the wedge is driven under the door, the more the door is raised.

The knife acts as a wedge, driving the carrot apart when it is struck with the hammer. It will also separate the carrot when used in a saw-like fashion, but it will take longer to accomplish the goal.

The shovel, when force is applied, will enter the ground with a parting movement.

Have the students complete the student experiment sheet. Ensure the students include a diagram.

| Part 1 | Part 2 | Part 3 |

The Wedge

Name: _____

Experiment One

I wonder: _____

_____

_____

I think: _____

_____

_____

I will: _____

_____

_____

_____

I saw: _____

_____

_____

_____

I learned: _____

_____

_____

SIMPLE MACHINES

The Wedge

Name: _____

Activity One

Color only the items on the page that use a wedge.

SIMPLE
MACHINES

The Screw

The **screw** is a simple machine that is similar to an inclined plane. It is made up of a **head**, a **shaft**, and a **pointed end**. The shaft has a cut going around and around it. This cut is called the **thread**. The screw fastens things together.

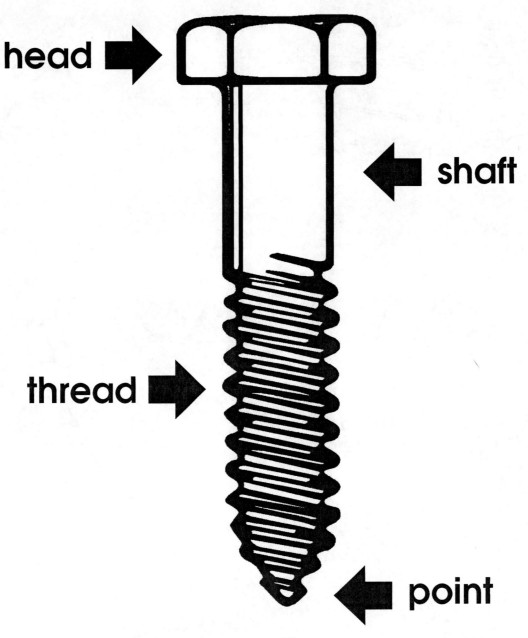

head ➡

⬅ shaft

thread ➡

⬅ point

SIMPLE
MACHINES

The Screw

A **bolt** is similar to a screw but has a flat end and works together with a **nut**. It also has a thread going around the shaft. A bolt fastens things together.

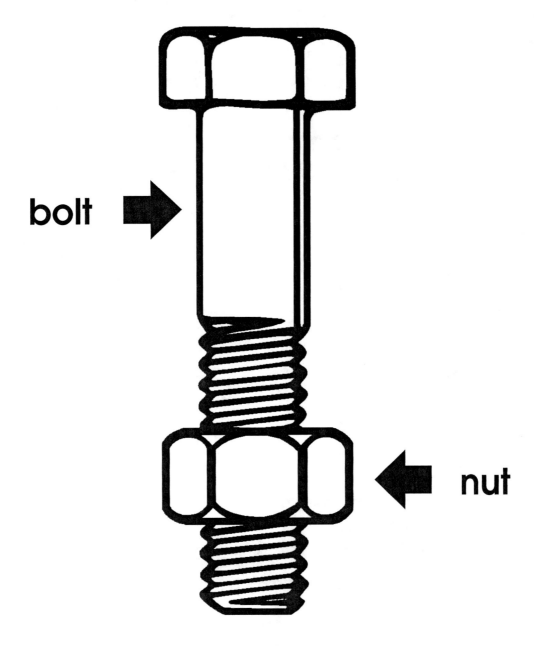

bolt

nut

The Screw

Name: _____

Activity One

Cut out the words below and paste each in the correct box.

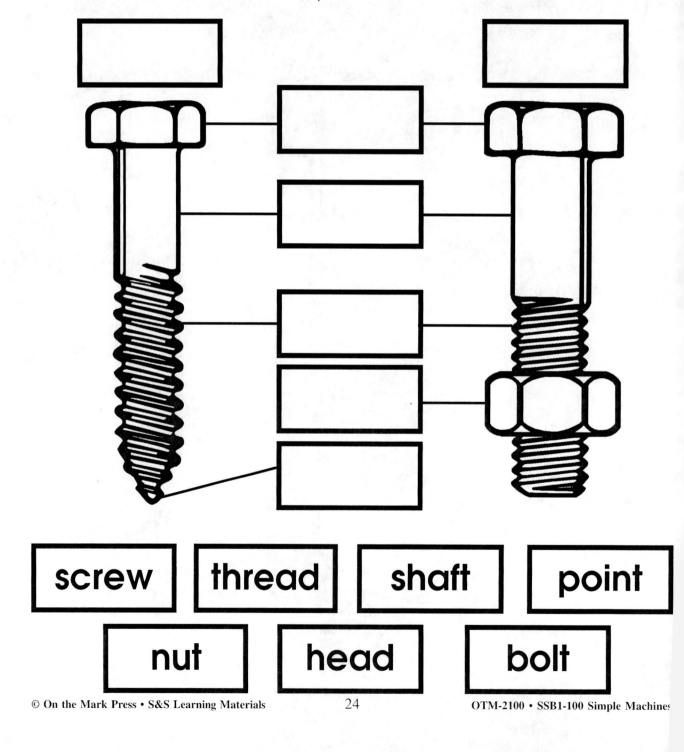

screw	thread	shaft	point

nut	head	bolt

The Screw

Activity Two

Cut out the triangle below, and roll it around your pencil or pen to create your own screw (an inclined plane wrapped around a shaft or pole).

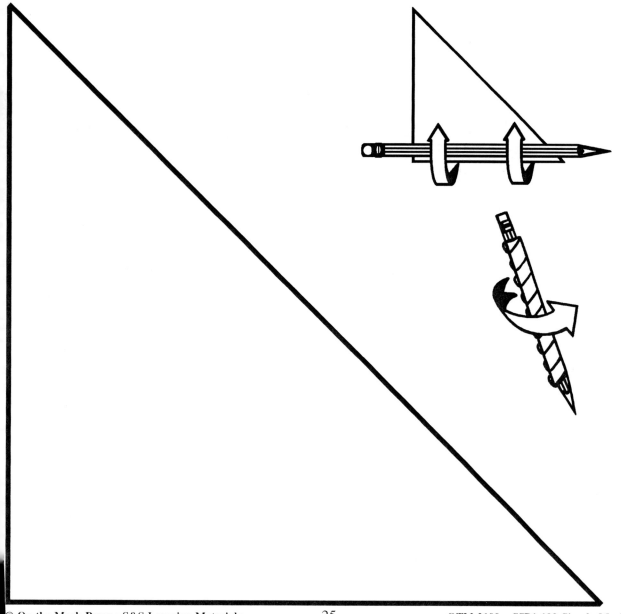

The Screw

Experiment One

Question: How do screws work?

Materials Required:
- wood screws (various sizes, lengths, heads)
- a block of soft wood
- various types of screwdrivers

Procedure:

1. Divide the class into small groups of two or three students.

2. Give each group one block of wood, and a variety of screws and screwdrivers.

3. Instruct the students to examine the screws and record their findings.

4. Turn the screws into the wood.

5. Count how many turns it takes to put the screw completely into the wood.

6. Record the results.

Conclusion: A greater number of turns will be required when using screws with a small pitch; however, the work will be easier.

Have the students complete the student experiment sheet. Include a diagram.

The Screw

Name: _____

Experiment One

Screw Observation Sheet		
Description	Picture	Number of Turns
Screw One		
Screw Two		
Screw Three		

The Screw

Name: _____

Experiment One

I wonder: _____

_____

_____

I think: _____

_____

_____

I will: _____

_____

_____

_____

I saw: _____

_____

_____

_____

I learned: _____

_____

_____

Levers

A **lever** is a simple machine that helps you to lift a large weight with very little effort. It is a bar that turns on a point called a fulcrum. When using a lever, there are three important parts. They are **effort**, **fulcrum**, and **load**.

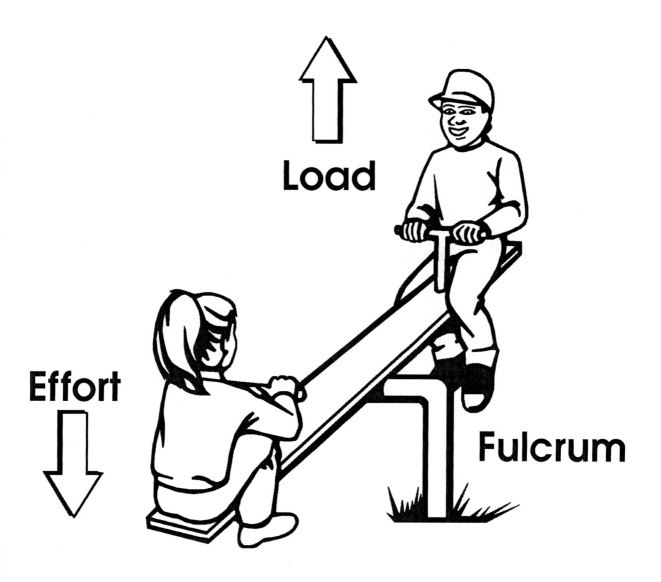

Load

Effort

Fulcrum

Levers

Name: _____

Activity One

Draw a picture of you and a friend on a seesaw. Write the words **load**, **effort**, and **fulcrum** where they belong on your picture.

SIMPLE MACHINES

Levers

Experiment One

Question: Do levers help to lift heavy things?

Materials Required:
- a wooden board (lever) approximately 120 cm (4 feet)
- a small wooden block (fulcrum)
- several heavy textbooks (load)

Procedure:
1. Place the wooden block on a flat, level surface.
2. Position the board on the block so that the board is balanced.
3. Place the textbooks on one end of the board (A).
4. Using your hand, press down (effort) the other end of the board (B) to lift the textbooks.
5. Describe the effort required to lift the textbooks.
6. Move the fulcrum in a direction away from the textbooks. Repeat steps 4 and 5.
7. Move the fulcrum in a direction toward the textbooks. Again, repeat steps 4 and 5.
8. Compete the student work sheet.

Conclusion: The effort required to lift the textbooks will be considerably less when the fulcrum is closer to the load.

Have the students complete the student experiment sheet. Have the students include a diagram.

Name: _____

Activity Two

Choose different objects in the classroom, and try to lift them using a board and a block of wood as a lever. Complete the chart below.

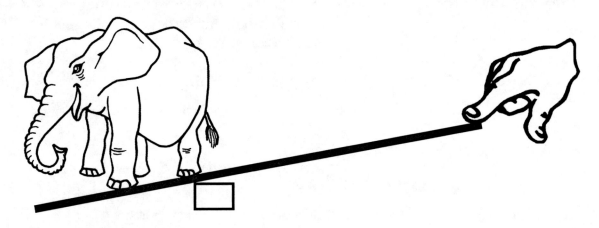

Name of object	How many?	Was lifting easy?

Levers

Experiment One

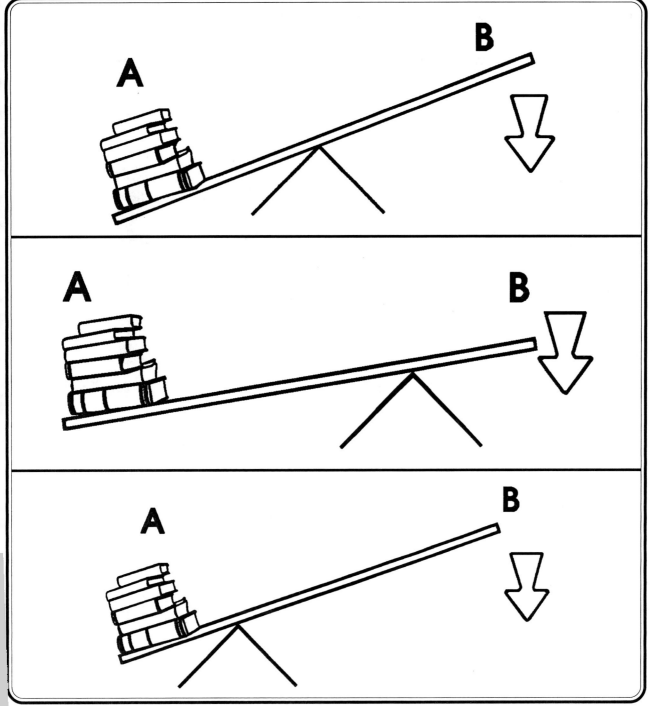

Levers

Name: _____

Experiment One

Draw a diagram showing the position of the **fulcrum**, the **effort**, and the **load**. Circle the appropriate number on the scale provided to describe the effort required to lift the textbooks.

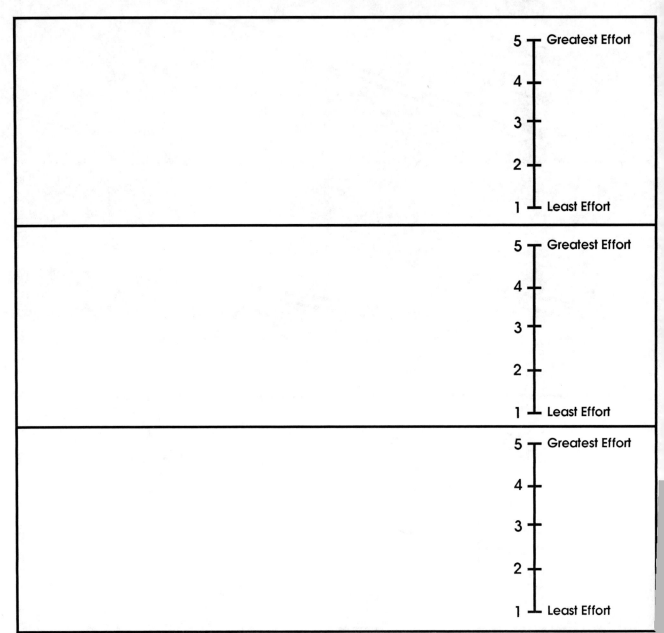

Levers

Name: _____

Experiment One

I wonder: _____

_____

_____

I think: _____

_____

_____

I will: _____

_____

_____

_____

I saw: _____

_____

_____

_____

I learned: _____

_____

_____

Levers

Name: _____

Activity Three

Color the pictures below and print the letter **F** where you think the fulcrum is found.

Levers

Name: _____

Activity Four

Color and show where the effort (**E**), load (**L**), and fulcrum (**F**) are found on the objects below.

The Pulley

A **pulley** is a form of lever. To lift an object, you need only to pull down on the rope. A system using more than one pulley is called a **block and tackle**. If you use a longer rope wrapped around more than one pulley, lifting will be even easier.

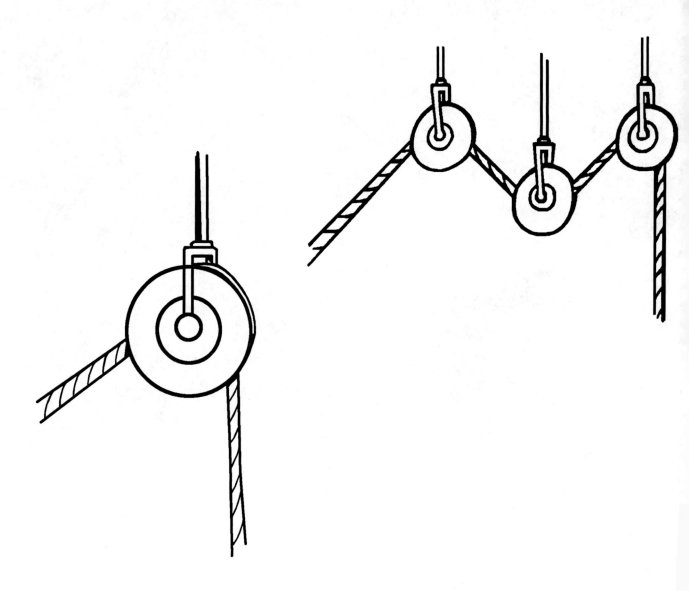

The Pulley

Activity One

Making a Spool Pulley

Materials Required:
- one clothes hanger (wire)
- one pair of wire cutters
- one spool (fishing line/thread/ribbon/wire)
- string or fishing line

Procedure:

1. Cut a length of wire from the clothes hanger.

2. Insert the wire through the hole in the spool and bend it into an oval shape making sure that the spool spins freely on the wire. Fasten the two ends of the wire by twisting them together. Use the wire cutters.

3. Place one end of the string on the spool and feed it through until there are equal lengths of string on each side of the spool.

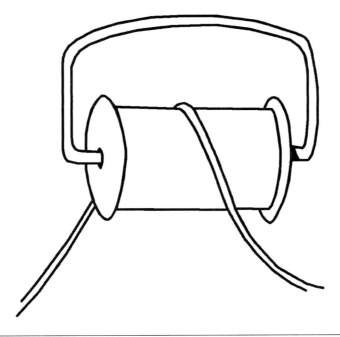

The Pulley

Experiment One

Question: Does a pulley make lifting easier?

Materials Required:
- a pulley with hook (spool pulley from Activity One)
- a pail with handle
- a spring scale
- two pieces of string (one short, one longer)
- a 0.5 to 1.0 kg (1 to 2 lb) weight

Procedure: **Part 1**

1. Fasten the short string to the pail handle.
2. Place the weight into the pail.
3. Attach the spring scale to the other end of the string.
4. Lift the pail up using only the spring scale.
5. Record the effort required to lift the pail as indicated on the scale.

Part 2

6. Fasten the pulley to an object located above eye-level (ceiling, tree branch, door jamb, playground equipment).
7. Place the longer string around the pulley and fasten one end to the pail handle.
8. Place the weight inside the pail.
9. Attach the spring scale to the other end of the string.
10. Lift the pail using only the scale by pulling down.
11. Record the effort required to lift the pail as indicated on the scale.

Conclusion: The recorded numbers from the spring scale will be very similar, but the students will notice that it is much easier pulling down (using a pulley) to lift an object thant it is to lift upward.

Have students complete the student experiment sheet.

Ensure the students include a diagram.

The Pulley

Experiment One

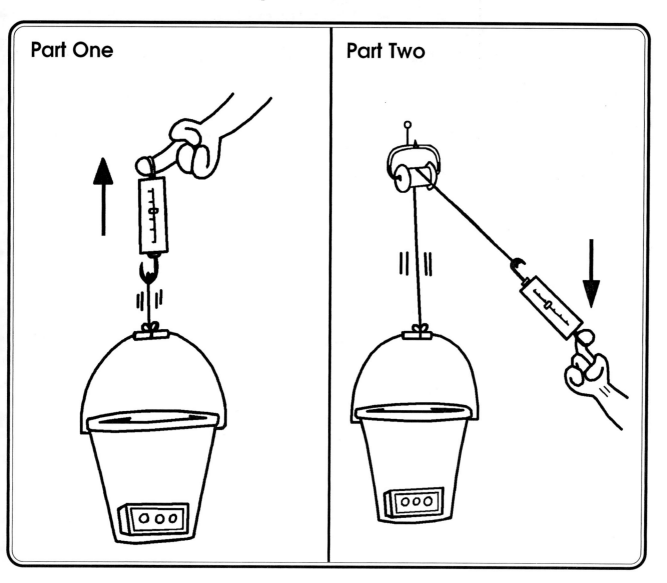

Part One

Part Two

The Pulley

Name: _____

Experiment One

Part One - Scale Reading	Part Two - Scale Reading
_____	_____
Part One	**Part Two**

The Pulley

Name: _____

Experiment One

I wonder: _____

_____

_____

I think: _____

_____

_____

I will: _____

_____

_____

_____

I saw: _____

_____

_____

_____

I learned: _____

_____

_____

SIMPLE MACHINES

The Pulley

Name: _____

Activity Two

Choose different objects in the classroom and try to lift them using your spool pulley. Complete the chart below.

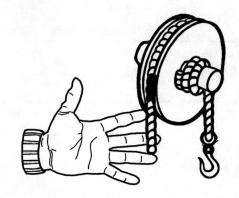

Name of object	How many?	Was lifting easy?

SIMPLE MACHINES

Wheel and Axle

Name: _____

A round type of lever is called a **wheel and axle**. The wheel turns around a small cylinder called an axle. A wheel and axle can help us lift and move heavy loads. Color the wheels and axles you see in the pictures below.

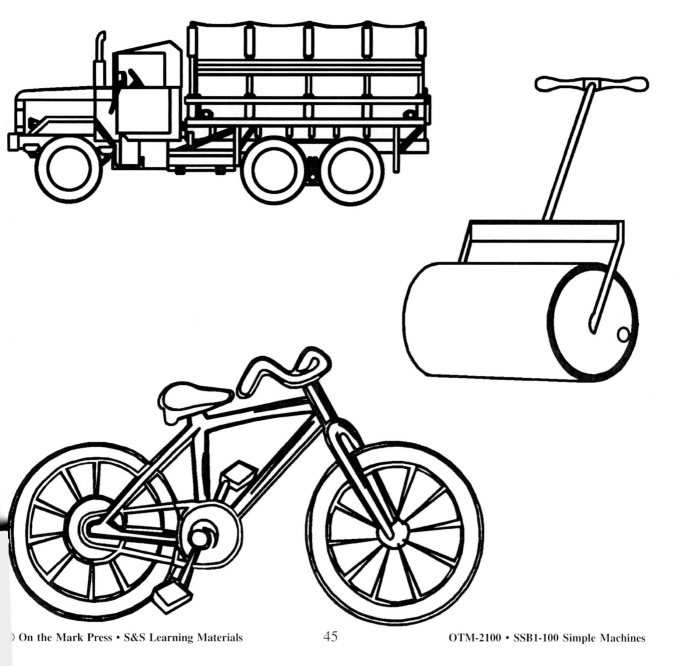

Wheel and Axle

Experiment One

Question: Which makes lifting easier: a larger wheel and axle, or a smaller wheel and axle?

Materials Required:
- one piece of dowel 2.5 cm (1 in) in diameter
- one piece of dowel, 5 cm (2 in) in diameter
- string, 100 cm (40 in) in length
- a pail
- a weight 0.5 to 1.0 kg (1 to 2 lbs)
- a marker

Procedure: Part 1

1. Fasten the string to the pail handle.

2. Place the weight into the pail.

3. Attach the other end of the string to the center of the 2.5-cm (1-in) dowel.

4. Using the marker, place a mark on the top side of the dowel.

5. Begin to roll the dowel in your hands, winding up the string and lifting the pail.

6. Count how many times the mark returns to the top of the dowel while you lift the pail to it.

7. Record your results on the student work sheet.

Part 2

8. Repeat steps 1 to 7 using the 5-cm (2-in) piece of dowel.

Conclusion: The students will find that the larger (diameter) dowel requires fewer turns to lift the pail, therefore making the work easier.

Have the students complete the student experiment sheet. Ensure the students include a diagram.

Wheel and Axle

Experiment One

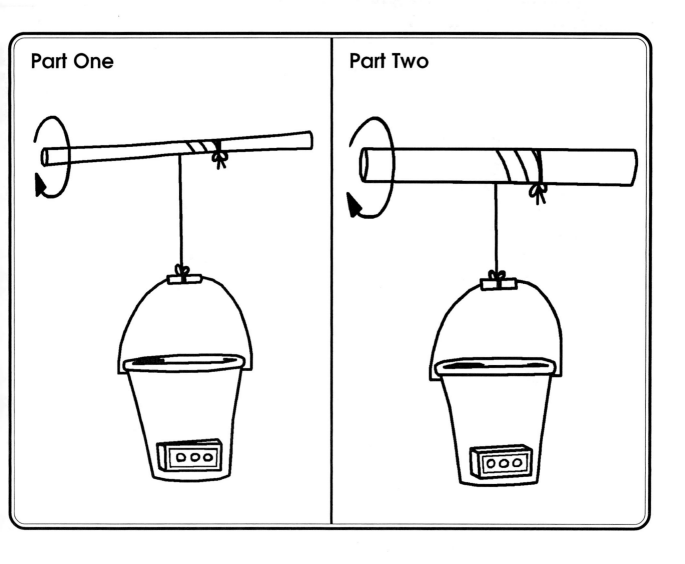

Part One

Part Two

Wheel and Axle

Name: _____

Experiment One

Part One - Number of Turns	Part Two - Number of Turns
_____	_____
Part One	**Part Two**

Wheel and Axle

Name: _____

Experiment One

I wonder: _____

_____

_____

I think: _____

_____

_____

I will: _____

_____

_____

_____

I saw: _____

_____

_____

_____

I learned: _____

_____

_____

Wheel and Axle

Name: _____

Activity One

Color the objects which use a wheel and axle.

Compound Machines

We use many simple machines each day. Sometimes they work together and are called a **compound machine**. For example, a bicycle is a compound machine because it is made up of **levers**, **wheels and axles**, **inclined planes**, **pulleys**, and **screws**.

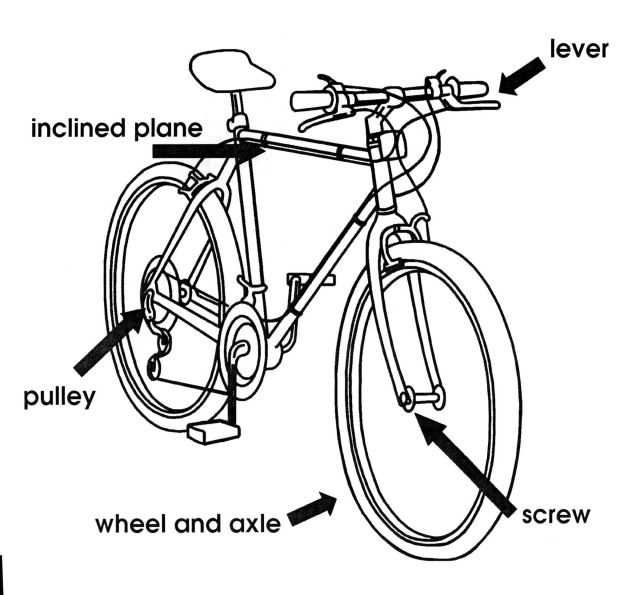

lever

inclined plane

pulley

wheel and axle

screw

Compound Machines

Name: _____

Activity One

Find and label six simple machines on the picture below. Color the picture.

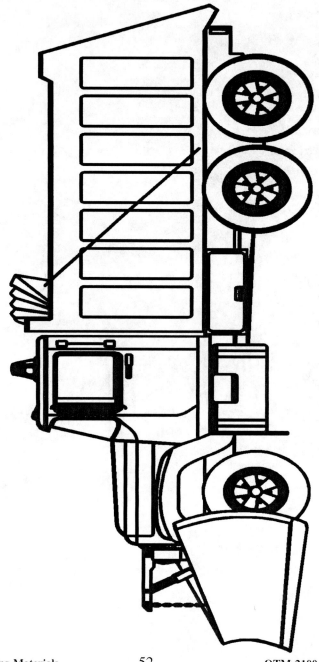

Simple Machines
Learning Log

Name: _____

Learning Log

Simple Machines

Think of two things that surprized you while learning about simple machines. Draw a picture of each one below.

SIMPLE MACHINES

Learning Log

Name: _____

Inclined Plane

1. What we did: _____

_____

_____

_____

2. What I learned: _____

_____

_____

_____

Learning Log

Name: _____

The Wedge

1. What we did: _____

_____

_____

_____

2. What I learned: _____

_____

_____

_____

Learning Log

Name: _____

The Screw

1. What we did: _____

_____

_____

_____

2. What I learned: _____

_____

_____

_____

Learning Log

Name: _____

Levers

1. What we did: _____

_____

_____

_____

2. What I learned: _____

_____

_____

_____

Learning Log

Name: _____

The Pulley

1. What we did: _____

_____

_____

_____

2. What I learned: _____

_____

_____

_____

Wheel and Axle

1. What we did: _____

   _____

   _____

   _____

2. What I learned: _____

   _____

   _____

   _____

Learning Log

Name: _____

Simple Machines

1. What we did: _____

_____

_____

_____

2. What I learned: _____

_____

_____

_____

Review

Name: _____

Activity One

Find and label the simple machines usded in the picture.

SIMPLE MACHINES

Review

Name: _____

Activity Two

shovel	rolling pin	point	compound machines
fulcrum	pulley	ramp	wheel and axle
lever	shaft	bicycle	inclined plane
seesaw	axle	bolt	wedge

Fill in each blank with the correct word from the word bank.

1. A sloping surface which allows an object to be moved from one elevation to another with less effort than lifting, is called an _____.

2. A _____ is an example of an inclined plane.

3. An inclined plane that moves is called a _____.

4. A _____ is an example of a wedge.

5. A screw is made up of a head at the top end, and a _____ at the bottom end. The _____ has a cut going around it that is called a thread.

6. A simple machine that is similar to a screw but works with a nut to fasten things together, is called a _____.

Name: _____

7. A _____ helps to lift a heavy weight with only a little effort.

8. A lever is a bar that turns on a point, called a _____.

9. A _____ is an example of a lever.

10. A type of lever that works with a rope is called a _____.

11. A _____ is a round type of lever. The wheel turns around a cylinder, called an _____.

12. A _____ uses a wheel and axle.

13. _____ are made up of a variety of simple machines.

14. A _____ is an example of a compound machine because it uses a lever, inclined plane, pulley, wheel and axle, and a screw.

Simple Machines

Name: _____

Follow-Up Activities and Work Sheets

Discovery Table

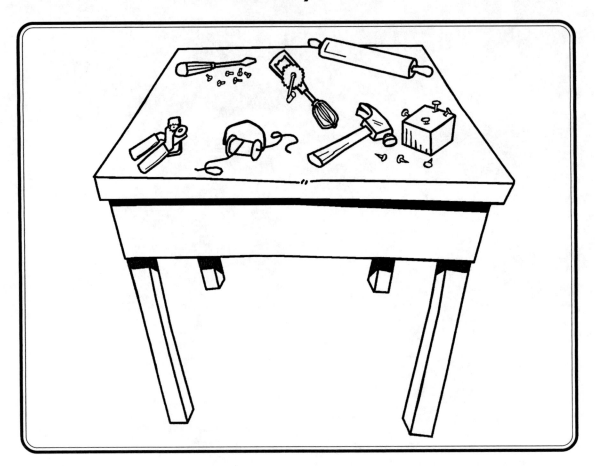

One of the most important methods of learning is through **discovery**. Place a table in your classroom to display various simple machines. Allow the students to experience firsthand how they feel, how they move, and how they work. Encourage the students to **experiment** with these simple machines and **create** compound machines. Identify the objects on the table for the students.

Be sure to promote safety in the classroom. Safety glasses should be worn by students while they are at the discovery table.

Follow-Up Activities and Work Sheets

Name: _____

Simple Machines at School

Tour the school and the schoolyard to identify simple machines. Complete the chart below.

Item Name	Location at School	Type of Simple Machine

Simple Machine ABC's

Draw a picture of a machine beginning with each letter of the alphabet. Print each name in the box.

A	B

C

D

E

F

G

H

I

J

K

L

M

N

O

P

Q

R

S

T

U

V

W

X

Y

Z

Follow-Up Activities and Work Sheets

Name: _____

Acrostic Poetry

Choose a tool or simple machine that you have studied. Write an acrostic poem about it. Each line of your poem should begin with a letter in the name of the tool or simple machine. Illustrate your poem on the back of this sheet.

Example: **L**ift heavy things
Enormous loads
Very helpful
Effort needed
Rulers can be levers
Simply great machine!

_____

_____

_____

_____

_____

_____

_____

_____

Follow-Up Activities and Work Sheets

Riddles

Cut out the riddle sheet below and fold on the dotted line. Write a riddle about a tool or machine on the front of the riddle page. Write the answer on the inside page and draw a picture of it.

Example: Riddle - I am a lever. I have one sharp end and one round end. You use me when you are thirsty. I fit in your hand. What am I?

Answer - can opener

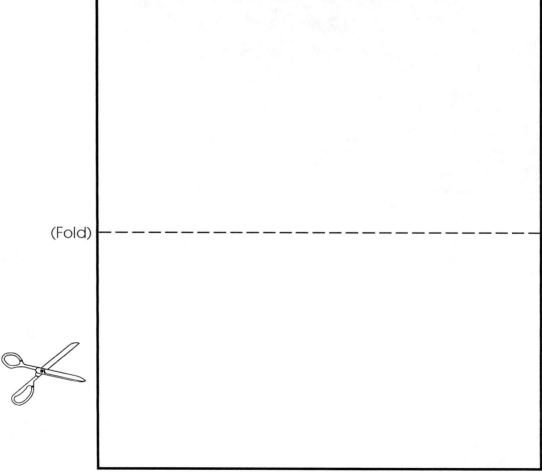

(Fold)

Machines of the Future

Draw a picture of your machine. Name your machine, and explain how it works and how it will help us in the future.

_____

_____

_____

_____

_____

Name: _____

Idea Web

Create an idea web. Write all the words you can think of in each oval that relate to the word it is connected to.

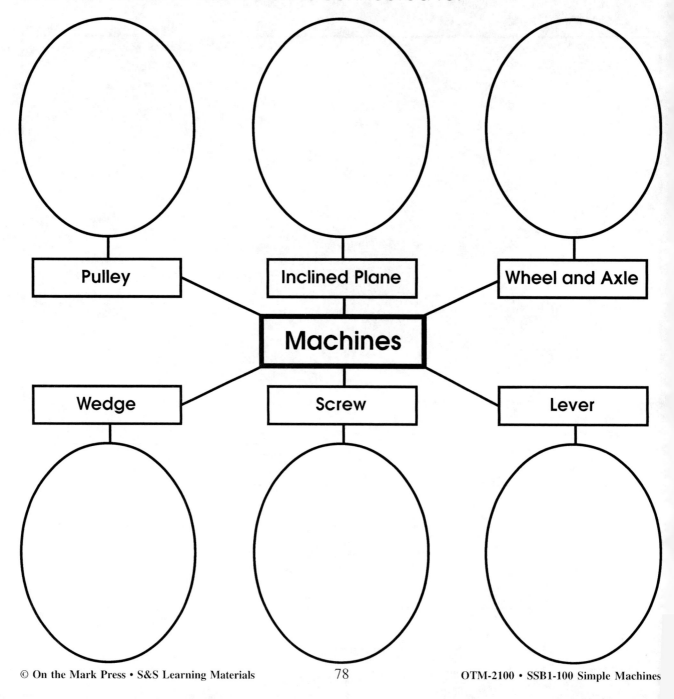

Follow-Up Activities and Work Sheets

Name: _____

Rhyming Words

For each of the simple machine words below, write down three rhyming words.

tool _____ _____ _____

wedge _____ _____ _____

simple _____ _____ _____

wheel _____ _____ _____

plane _____ _____ _____

screw _____ _____ _____

head _____ _____ _____

lever _____ _____ _____

Follow-Up Activities and Work Sheets

Create a Collage

Divide your class into six groups and assign each group one simple machine. Provide old magazines, catalogs and newspaper flyers. Have the students find pictures of the simple machines you have assigned to them. Instruct them to cut out the pictures, glue them onto the sheet provided, and label each one. You may wish to assemble the sheets into a Simple Machines Book, or display them together on a large sheet of cardboard or bulletin board. Allow the groups an opportunity to share their work with the class.

Follow-Up Activities and Work Sheets

Tracing Patterns

Reproduce the pictures provided below. Ask the students to trace these shapes. They may be used in a variety of ways, such as creating a patterning page or a tool collage.

Follow-Up Activities and Work Sheets

Name: _____

Crossword Puzzle

Across

1. used to join things together
3. a machine with more than one simple machine
6. the support on which a lever rests
9. something you can use to do work
10. A _____ separates or lifts.

Down

2. a test to discover something
4. a small wheel and rope
5. give it your best try
7. a bar which turns on a fulcrum
8. An inclined plane is a _____ machine.

Follow-Up Activities and Work Sheets

Name: _____

Word Search

axle	compound	effort
fulcrum	invention	lever
load	machine	plane
pulley	screw	simple
tool	wedge	wheel

```
I  N  V  E  N  T  I  O  N  Z  G  V
C  O  M  P  O  U  N  D  Z  Y  B  V
F  U  L  C  R  U  M  L  C  W  R  V
P  U  L  L  E  Y  A  X  L  E  F  X
W  H  E  E  L  S  C  R  E  W  K  N
B  D  V  E  D  Y  H  F  X  F  C  I
Q  Z  E  Q  D  S  I  M  P  L  E  G
X  T  R  P  L  A  N  E  I  L  Y  I
F  P  W  E  D  G  E  F  F  O  R  T
U  B  Y  N  G  P  W  Y  D  A  H  O
N  G  H  P  X  H  T  W  J  D  J  O
I  Q  S  D  N  K  Q  O  E  T  H  L
```

Invention Fair

Dear Parent/Guardian,

Your child/children will soon be participating in an **Invention Fair**. It is designed to promote creative problem-solving, and encourage independent thinking skills. The students will follow a sequential process to invent a new product or develop a new method of completing a task.

We will begin by discussing existing inventions. This will allow the children to gain an appreciation for the invention process.

It is necessary for the children to first find an idea for an invention. You may be asked if you need a new product, or if you require a new method to solve a problem or to lessen your workload. Your participation and encouragement will make the children's experience a positive one.

During the actual process of inventing and building, the children may need to be reminded that many inventors have met with failure along the way. Your interest and encouragement will ensure that this science experience if unforgettable!

Inventions are required at school on_____ .

Sincerely,

Invention Fair

Invention Ideas

"I don't know what to do. I can't think of anything."

The following list of invention ideas are to be used to motivate and encourage young inventors.

- a new bird feeder
- a new container
- a new pencil case
- a new clothing design
- a new toy
- a new recipe
- a new book bag
- a new musical instrument
- a new board game
- a new cleaning tool
- a new product for pets
- a new toothbrush holder

Invention Fair

Name: _____

Name of Invention: _____

Materials Required: _____

_____

_____

_____

_____

How did you make your invention? _____

_____

_____

_____

_____

_____

How will it work or be used?

_____

_____

_____

_____

_____

SIMPLE MACHINES

Invention Fair

Name: _____

Invention Sketch

Complete a diagram of your invention.

Invention Fair

Name: _____

Invention Conference Form

Inventor _____ Grade _____

Invention _____

Originality

| 5 | 10 | 15 | 20 | 25 |

Effort/Completion

| 5 | 10 | 15 | 20 | 25 |

Written Report

| 5 | 10 | 15 | 20 | 25 |

Oral Presentation

| 5 | 10 | 15 | 20 | 25 |

Total Score _____

Judged by _____

SIMPLE
MACHINES

Certificate

Excellence in Science Award

has successfully completed the unit on

Simple Machines

Congratulations!

_____
Teacher

_____
Date

Simple

Machines

Grouping

Classroom Groups

SIMPLE MACHINES

Conference Form

Name: _____   Date: _____

Activity Title	Rating 1 - very poor 2 - poor 3 - good 4 - very good 5 - excellent	Comments
	1 2 3 4 5	
	1 2 3 4 5	
	1 2 3 4 5	
	1 2 3 4 5	
	1 2 3 4 5	
	1 2 3 4 5	
	1 2 3 4 5	
	1 2 3 4 5	
	1 2 3 4 5	
	1 2 3 4 5	
	1 2 3 4 5	
	1 2 3 4 5	
	1 2 3 4 5	
	1 2 3 4 5	
	1 2 3 4 5	
	1 2 3 4 5	
	1 2 3 4 5	
	1 2 3 4 5	
	1 2 3 4 5	
	1 2 3 4 5	

Student's Signature: _____   Teacher's Signature: _____

SIMPLE MACHINES

Experiment

I wonder: _____

_____

_____

I think: _____

_____

_____

I will: _____

_____

_____

_____

I saw: _____

_____

_____

_____

I learned: _____

_____

_____

Brainstorming

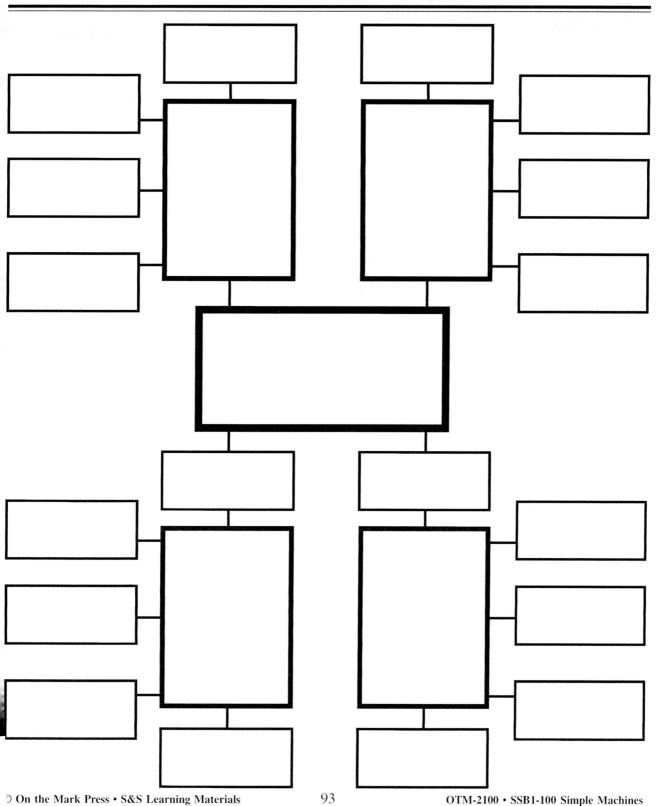

Answer Key

Wedge Activity: *(page 21)*
The following pictures should be colored:

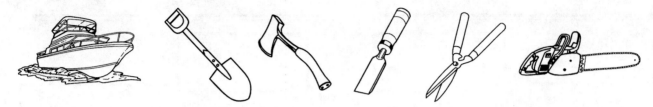

Screw Activity One: *(page 24)*

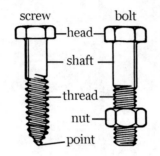

Levers Activity Three: *(page 36)*

Levers Activity Four: *(page 37)*

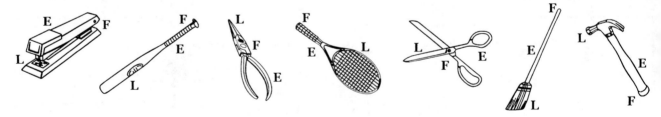

Wheel and Axle Activity One: *(page 50)*
The following objects should be colored:

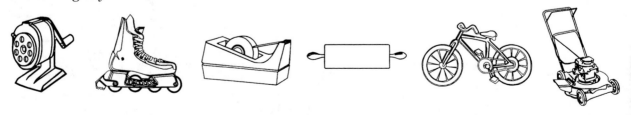

Compound Machines Activity: *(page 52)*

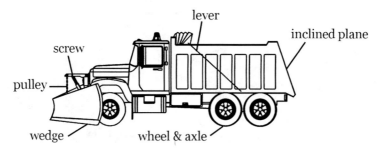

Review Activity One: *(page 62)*

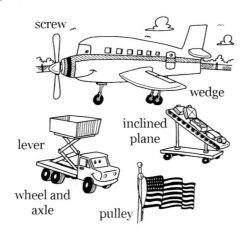

Review Activity Two: *(page 63)*

1. inclined plane		**2.** ramp		**3.** wedge	
4. shovel		**5.** point, shaft		**6.** bolt	
7. lever		**8.** fulcrum		**9.** seesaw	
10. pulley		**11.** wheel and axle, axle		**12.** rolling pin	
13. Compound machines		**14.** bicycle			

Crossword Puzzle: *(page 82)*

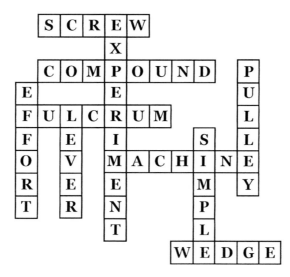

Word Search: *(page 83)*

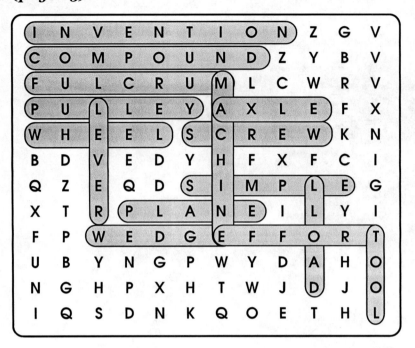

```
I  N  V  E  N  T  I  O  N  Z  G  V
C  O  M  P  O  U  N  D  Z  Y  B  V
F  U  L  C  R  U  M  L  C  W  R  M
P  U  L  L  E  Y  A  X  L  E  F  X
W  H  E  E  L  S  C  R  E  W  K  N
B  D  V  E  D  Y  H  F  X  F  C  I
Q  Z  E  Q  D  S  I  M  P  L  E  G
X  T  R  P  L  A  N  E  I  L  Y  I
F  P  W  E  D  G  E  F  F  O  R  T
U  B  Y  N  G  P  W  Y  D  A  H  O
N  G  H  P  X  H  T  W  J  D  J  O
I  Q  S  D  N  K  Q  O  E  T  H  L
```

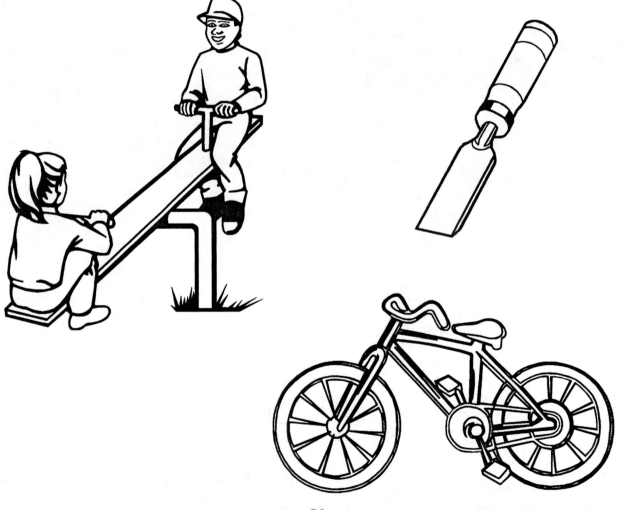